SEVEN CYCLES TO PROSPERITY

HOW TO CREATE WEALTH WITH YOUR CURRENT INCOME

(THE SEVEN FOLD ALCHEMIST METHOD)

Harvey Somanje

ACKNOWLEDGEMENT

This book has come about as a fruit of sixteen years of learning, failing, almost succeeding, perseverance through hard times a lots of patience culminating into success. I was never alone through this long journey; I am so grateful to my parents and siblings for their support. Mum and dad, thanks for still housing and feeding me when I was getting started on my entrepreneurial journey; even when the chips were down. To my mother-in-law; thanks for your continued support, you're a blessing.

Much thanks to my mentor and pastor the Late Prophet Kobus Van Rensburg who selflessly deposited much life treasures in me. I cannot forget my Financial mentor Lucas Hatingh; you are a beacon of light in dark times. Thank you for your great advice and mentorship.

Last but not least; my lovely wife Sandra; thanks for standing by my side through thick and thin. It's a pleasure travelling this road with you babe, I love you.

Table of Contents

INTRODUCTION

As with anything in life that is worth doing, building a secure financial future for yourself and your family is a process. For some people, it is fast and meteoric but for the vast majority it is like running a marathon; slow and painful at times, but still rewarding at the end. Regardless of how your personal road has been, there are some very important questions that you need to answer when it comes to building wealth. It simply boils down to answering some hard questions; what? How? and where? What to do to get wealthy, how to go about building it, Where are you going and Where do you start?

There is a plethora of books on what to do, fewer books on where to start and a reasonable number on how to go about doing it. There is plenty in this world that someone can do to get income so that makes the "what" part easier to answer. It is comforting to know that no matter where you are in the world there are plenty of challenges that present opportunities for enterprising individuals to make a living. The challenge lays in the *"how"* part. How to go about building wealth? This book aims to mainly answer two questions; where to start and how to build wealth. I will leave the "what" part to your creative genius to figure out.

In a world where everyone is trying to make their own way to success, make a mark and embrace their own individuality, things may seem complicated. The truth of the matter is that it really isn't that complicated at all; the same old principles of success apply today as they always have. We all just put our own spin to the same old basic principles. You can find comfort in the knowledge that; things are not as difficult as they seem because there really is nothing new under the sun (except for technology of course). Let me put it this way; the wheel has been working perfectly well since it was invented. Nobody can reinvent the wheel. All we do is take the same old wheel and develop our own brand of Tyres; that is what we call "making our own mark."

My personal journey towards financial abundance started some 16 years ago when I registered my first company at the age of 22. I wish I could brag about how I aimed for the stars and dreamt big at such a young age but no; it was hard. I have watched my hard-earned money go up in smoke and my dreams reduced to cinder. I have started over at least five times; cried often and well... pulled myself up by my bootstraps... literary. It's been a long journey; I have learnt a thing or two along the way. I have suffered loss several times before finally starting to win. I don't give myself credit for having found new hidden wisdom though; it's the same age-old wisdom which has been around since the world began. I just learnt to apply it and I hope that by laying it out in this book I may help a fellow traveler find the road a little easier.

I have found much inspiration from nature; let's face it, natural is best. It is from nature that I learnt the seven cycles to prosperity or just to be fancy I can call it; "The seven-fold Alchemy method". I have also done my best to lay down some of the most important lessons I've learnt over the years. I want to share with you this simple yet powerful formula that I learnt much later in life. It has really transformed my personal finances and has made structuring finances a lot easier.

From time to time I will quote from the Holy Bible which is the most ancient and sacred of all books with pages full of ageless wisdom and I also quoted other authors whose work I have had the privilege of reading.

x

CHAPTER 1
Laying the foundation

There are many reasons why we all need financial abundance and the acquisition of wealth. Whatever the reason or motivation, it is comforting to know that finances work pretty much the same way they always have since the beginning. There is no new truth; only the same old truth and principles that have been around for ages. I dare say; there is no secret to wealth; otherwise, no one would acquire it.

The knowledge is all around us; I have seen people with very little or no formal education get extremely wealthy while the educated elite struggle financially. Perhaps that is why we have so much corruption in Africa; the educated elite don't know how to build wealth so they steal it – no pointing fingers or naming names.

The truth of the matter is that, anything that can be taught can be learnt. No subject has had so much attention in recent years as the subject of personal finances. There have been more books written on personal finances in the last 20 years than at any time in the history of publishing. Why is that? I believe it is time for multitudes to finally partake in the abundant feast of wealth. The best part is that there is enough to go around.

My personal journey to acquire wealth started back in 2002. I was only 21 years old at the time with no experience whatsoever. To me, wealth could be attributed to good fortune or as a reward for faithful religious devotion. I remember how as a young Christian I heard sermons for years on how; giving money and tithing to the church is the silver bullet for killing off poverty, lack, and all financial ills. Boy, I was in for a surprise.

Being a preacher boy, I even developed up a few sermons of my own along those lines actually. But as I watched time pass by, month by month, year after year, I could only but dream of making it financially. I realized that I needed to learn more about finances than I grew up knowing and that was when my personal education on finances started. I guess when the student is ready, the teacher does appear. My first cue was when I found John Maxwell book *"The 21 irrefutable laws of leadership"* in someone's trash can. The only time I ever found something valuable in a trash can I might add. My re-education had started, a long string of books followed; somehow magically finding their way into my hands. I remember the time; I wanted to buy a computer from a friend. I had paid the deposit but instead of reserving the computer, he decided to sell the computer to somebody else. Bad, I know. After much back and forth and I realized there is no way I would get all my money back; I asked him to give me any cash he had at hand and any item of equal value and we'd be squared. That he did, so instead of a sour deal we kind of became friends. One day he asked me if I had ever heard of "rich dad, poor dad" of course I had never heard of it. To cut the long story short, he shared the audiobook with me and I was well on my way to further financial education.

Earlier I did mention that before then, the only thing I knew about financial prosperity was giving to the church and alms. Now don't get me wrong; Giving tithes, offerings and alms have a very important place in the establishment of your financial security. But these practices alone are not the only things that will prosper you. There is more to the subject.

I have seen many deeply religious, good people disoriented after years of good deeds as to why their generosity is not being rewarded justly. Let's not get into religious politics so I'll just stop there. On the other hand, we have very hard-working employees who spend their lives doing the best they can in the hope that wealth will one day appear in their lives at the appointed time... it's usually a very long wait. One which usually ends with a fat retirement cheque, ill-advised investment, and poof! Money gone, depression sets in.

Think of finances like building a house; first, you dig the foundation; lay the foundation and then you build the walls of the house. Roof the house, do the interior and exterior finishing touches, then you furnish the place. Each and every stage of building is important. One stage cannot replace another; each aspect adds value to the building. An ancient nugget of wisdom I have always cherished is found in the Holy bible;

"Through wisdom is a house built; by understanding it is established:

And by knowledge shall the chambers be filled with all precious and pleasant riches." Proverbs 24:3-4 KJV

Think of giving as part of the foundation in your relationship with money. What you cannot give away has mastery over you. The point of financial abundance is to have command over vast amounts of money. You have to be master over the money, not a slave to your wealth. If you can give away money to a good cause you have taken the first step on the journey to not only fulfillment and happiness but also to great wealth. I have found that the biggest problem with the topic of money is not money but the emotions attached to money. The emotions range from ecstasy to crippling fear. Think of how many people are on an emotional high on payday. They slowly sink to the lowest point mid-month before coming out of depression on payday again.

Giving money follows the natural law of reciprocity. When you give out, it returns to you in abundance. When you sow you reap. Still; let us remember that although the journey of a thousand miles starts with one step… the journey does not end with the single step; it continues with the second, third step and so on and so forth.

According to layman's definition; riches are accumulated precious possessions. These possessions may be material, emotional, spiritual etc. Bottom line they are gathered together and ascribed to a person, family or community. This brings me to the next most important aspect of a strong financial foundation; learn to accumulate money.

When I first heard of the concept of "paying yourself first" I was excited but totally missed the point because I thought it meant "spend on yourself first"; this I did and lavishly so I might add. It's funny now and you may laugh. It wasn't until I read the book; *The richest man in Babylon* by George Samuel Clasons that I finally understood that it meant I must save not less than ten percent of my income for myself.

It was hard at first as I would feel guilty to be amassing money while there were so many needs around me… and in my own life primarily. But soon I began to see that giving and saving money are like two sides of the same coin. The one side to keep me humble, the other side to elevate me… "Brings balance to the force."

So I persisted and pushed beyond the initial guilt. Once I learnt the lesson, I then always had money; well at least 10% of all my income, I felt motivated to work harder and to save more because now I had a seed for my coming prosperity and riches.

I've seen and heard many people talk about the great things they are planning to do and the great things they are going to do by faith. The question I always ask is; "have you saved any money for it?" if the answer is yes, I know they will make it beyond the dreaming phase. If the answer is no; it is one indication that the dream is not powerful enough to demand a portion of their hard-earned money to be set aside… **their thirst is greater than their quest.**

Proverbs 21:20 GNB "Wise people live in wealth and luxury, but stupid people spend their money as fast as they get it."

This portion of scripture shows two contrasting mindsets; that of a poor person and that of a rich person. Now some may argue that nobody ever gets get rich by saving money… true! But nobody ever starts getting rich without first learning to possess money either. Saving money gives a person the opportunity to master the desire for wasteful, needy living and frivolous spending.

I believe that the true test for character is when you have the money you can spend but you chose not to spend it. Developing such a character early is very important. You may need to help yourself keep the discipline by living on a strict budget; do what you need to do to stay the course.

Are you familiar with the story of Joseph the Hebrew boy who became Prime minister of ancient Egypt at the height of Egyptian civilization?

Pharaoh had a dream which Joseph interpreted that it meant there was a famine coming to sweep across the land after seven years of abundance. Pharaoh asks for his counsel and Joseph's advice was simple; "Start a savings plan", he said. "Save 20% of all crops".

Sure enough, after seven years there was famine all across the land and Egypt ends up with the wealth of the whole region. I wonder what could have happened if Joseph had recommended a day of prayer and fasting for rain to continue.

CHAPTER 2
What about my debts

I grew up in what was then called *"a third world country"*, I believe the politically correct term now is "developing countries". I am from a country called Malawi, in central Africa. It's a beautiful landlocked country with one of the biggest freshwater lakes in the world. By the age of 10; we would occasionally hear on the news over the radio that some European nations or the World Bank had forgiven our country its debt of so many millions of dollars. It would seem the whole nation collectively sighed in relief and then the news anchor would read the next news item which would normally be; "His Excellency the President is seeking further economic aid for our nation…" the cycle continued.

I am by no means bad-mouthing Africa, am simply trying to demonstrate that debt is a vice; almost like gambling or smoking. It has a way to keep you coming for more. Several generations after independence most African nations still haven't shaken off the shackles of debt and poverty.

Now as a person trying to build wealth, how do you do go about accumulating wealth with an enemy such as debt breathing down your neck trying to keep you under. There is a very interesting story in the Holy Bible about a Jew who lived during the time just after the Babylonian exile. He was a cupbearer to the king in the Persian Palace. Looks like hostile takeover is not a new thing really; first, the Babylonians took his people captive, and then the Medes and Persians took over from them…

His name was Nehemiah. To cut the long story short, he had a vision to rebuild the war-ravaged city of Jerusalem. He got permission from the King and he went and mobilized the people to start rebuilding the city. Partway into the project, opposition arose from the neighboring tribes.

It came to a point where the other tribes threatened to attack and scatter the Jews so they don't complete the work of rebuilding the once magnificent city.

Now they were faced with some choices;

1. **Stop building to concentrate on fighting a war to defend their territory.**

2. **Ignore the threats and try to build as fast as they could.**

3. **Stop building, run away from the fight and leave the city in ruins.**

Nehemiah opted for option number four; build and defend.

"They which built on the wall, and they that bare burdens, with those that laded, everyone with one of his hands wrought in the work, and with the other hand held a weapon.

For the builders, everyone had his sword girded by his side, and so built. And he that sounded the trumpet was by me". Nehemiah 4:17-18 KJV

So many times finances and life feel like war... rightfully so. If money wasn't important, we wouldn't spend as much time as we do on the matter. Sure it's just a way of keeping score but it sulks when your scorecard is in the red. Sometimes you have to fight with one hand and build with the other. If debt is an enemy you're dealing with, fight it off and build at the same time. Now situations are not the same for everyone; others may be facing emotional, physical and spiritual or relationship debt. Whatever the challenge, instead of burying yourself in the business or career, how about mastering the art of being a building warrior?

Life is never fair, sometimes it gives us a handful, a mouth full or generally more than we can handle. Sometimes we bite off more than we can chew but regardless of the sequence of events leading to the current situation we all have to fight on many fronts at times. If you're lucky you may only have to fight on two fronts… that's just life.

I watched the movie Thor for the 99th time a few weeks ago and I remember the scene when Thor walks into the Asgardian hall to a standing ovation at the beginning of the movie "Thor". His father "Oden" addressing the young warrior prince who is so engrossed with his day of recognition; "Thor… I have entrusted you with the hammer Mjolnir forged from the heart of a dying star. A fitting companion for a King, it can be used as a tool for building or as a weapon for destruction…"

Many times, the same tool we need for building is the tool we need to use to keep our enemies at bay or what the heck; demolish them.

I think the best advice about getting out of debt that I've ever heard is from George Clason's book "The richest man in Babylon". He recommends using 20% of your income to service debts and never forget to save 10% of your income. In essence, live on 70% of your income. Knowing I am not one to reinvent the wheel, I would recommend the same.

Debt by its very nature is not just an issue of numbers; it's more intricate than that. It has a lot to do with stress, credibility, reputation, and relationship. There are times when people's relationships are broken over unpaid debt regardless of the amount. Debt can be stressful; which means you may not be at your best creatively when the burden of debt is hanging heavily over you. I have heard many fellow Christians pray for supernatural debt cancellation and am sure it feels good when it happens. I for one prefer a more hands-on approach. It's a fight; you need to roll your sleeves up for and get to business. I must point out here that sometimes when used wisely debt can be a powerful ally in the endeavor to build wealth.

For example; there was a time I needed to invest in a business opportunity. I had very little money at hand so I used a credit card to buy stock and sell at a profit. I would then repay the credit card debt and add part of the profit I had made to order the next batch. Initially, the amount I had borrowed on credit card constituted 75% of my capital. On the second order, the amount I borrowed on credit card amount [which was the same as the previous time] constituted 50% of the capital.

I kept repeating the process until the amount borrowed from the credit card [which still remained the same by the way] should constitute 2% of my capital. At which point I would no longer need to borrow money from the credit card; I found a way to make friends with the enemy.

I know that credit card debt has been the undoing of many, but I suppose if you use a credit card as a mercenary army to fight your war; it may be a little friendlier. Otherwise, credit card debt is a very bad party guest, that's for sure.

Just to give you a clear idea what am talking about; this is what I did;

First order

Cash at hand	$100
Credit card loan amount	<u>$300</u>
Total	**$400**
Sale Turnover @50% profit	$600
Credit card loan	-$300
Cash in hand [not all profit]	**$300**

Second order

Cash at hand	$300
Credit card loan amount	<u>$300</u>
Total	**$600**
Sale Turnover @50% profit	$900
Less credit card loan	$300
Cash at hand [not all profit]	**$600**

Third order

Cash at hand	$600

Credit card loan amount	<u>$300</u>
Total	**$900**
Sale turnover @ 50% profit	$1,350
Less credit card loan	$300
Cash at hand [not all profit]	**1,050**

Forth order

Cash at hand	1,050
Credit card loan amount	<u>$300</u>
Total	**$1,350**
Sale turnover @ 50% profit	$2,025
Less credit card loan	$300
Cash at hand [not all profit]	**$1,725**

Note: Of course my original $100 had to be deducted at some point because it is money I invested. For purposes of this illustration, I haven't done that. In actual fact, I did leave my initial investment of $100 in the business until it had multiplied it many times over.

After just four cycles of strict discipline to feed the business; I created $1,725 using my $100 and $300 I could borrow from the credit card. In the first cycle debt was 75% of my investment, by the fifth order debt was 14.81% of my capital.

I made it a point to promptly pay the credit card debt so I can have access to it again.

Lucky for me, I did not have many personal bills to pay at the time; my expenditure was covered by whatever little money I was making aside from the investment.

Would I recommend building a business on credit card debt? Not at all; the only reason I took that route was because, I had pre-orders to deliver and the customers had made a financial commitment to buy the stock. In other words, it was a calculated risk. Unfortunately after sometime I became overly-optimistic, extended credit facility to untrust-worthy customers… wipeout! It's a perilous world we live in.

If you are going to try credit card debt for investment, either have a job or another source on income that can cover the debt. Otherwise, build up savings, invest, then grow the investment from your profits. Expanding a business too quickly can bring the house crumbling down. Think of a fruit tree, it sheds its fruit and leaves and the very leaves and fruit that decorated its branches become fertilizer that makes the tree grow stronger. Growing a business organically has its perks but that my friend is a topic for another chapter.

CHAPTER 3
Building wealth: employ your money

Having saved at least 10% of your income for a while; the next step in the evolution is to find your money profitable occupation. There are a lot of books on the subject, countless opinions on how to select a profitable investment/employment for your money and needless to say you probably have some fantastic idea you've been nursing for a while that promises to be the Holy Grail to cure all your financial ills.

Before you pour your hard-earned money into any chalice allow me to share one word of wisdom that has rescued me from near disaster once or twice. Here goes; "Nobody will pay you for following your passion; people will pay you for following their passion". It may sound conflicting but it really isn't. It simply means that your customers are the ones who sustain your business. If they don't like your product you are going nowhere, no matter how passionate you are about the product. If other people love your product; you have a business.

For years I worked on a business idea to market the sport of basketball in my home country- Malawi. It's a sport that I am passionate about, I had great, nay, brilliant ideas on how to elevate the sport. There was only one problem; 98% percent of sports fans in the country [including basketball players] love soccer. The media is devoted to soccer. It wasn't long before I realized I had no business and my money was gone. Sleepless nights ensued… early midlife crisis commenced. Lucky for me I was only 22 years old, there was still time to recover.

That's when I learnt that one should only invest in their passion only if it is also someone else's passion. It's just logical; Supplier – Product – Consumer. There has to be a sizeable consumer base for your product for it to qualify as a viable business idea.

Now, we all know that the world is evolving at a rapid pace and things we never realized we even needed come on the market and we all ask ourselves; "how did we ever live without this?" so there is a fine line somewhere in there between your passion turning out to be a hobby or a business. Nobody knew we need social media, now we can't live without it… literary. If falls on you to do the research.

CHAPTER 4
The three-strand cord of business

As I said earlier on, there are many ways through which money can be made. Most people usually ask the question; "what is the best investment portfolio that can grow my money?" That my friend is a good question that has practically made a fortune for consultancy firms, stock brokers and investment gurus. To be honest I don't know everything about stocks and bonds and other fancy investment vehicles. There is just one universal truth when it comes to multiplying money; there has to be a business transaction involving buying or making a product at a lower price and selling it at a higher price. The difference between the later and the former is profit. It's simple enough but not always easy. When it comes to making money, the best way as far as I am concerned is to start a business. You need to own a business which is the vehicle that will bring you the profit you so desire. Whether you own all of the business or part of the business, it doesn't matter; you just need to own a business. The reason you need to own a business is because you have a level of control over the outcome compared to other avenues where you put your money and hope the company does well or the currency maintains its value or even that the government maintains a particular policy. Owning a business gives you control over how much money you can make.

Let's take a moment to look at the bare bones of what makes the skeletal structure of a business. There are three things that are necessary to make a business, the three-cord rope of business so to speak.

1. **A problem.**

2. **Solution**

3. **Customers/market niche that is willing to pay for the solution.**

Without a problem, you cannot even talk of business. Thank God our lives are full of problems. First, you need to identify a problem worth solving. Every successful business solves a particular problem. Mobile phone businesses solve a communication and information processing problem to a certain degree. Supermarkets solve a hunger problem, Baby sitters solve time and family raising problem. Every business solves a particular problem. Highly successful businesses solve problems that really need to be solved. Just think of the medical and health care industry; it solves a problem nobody dares to ignore, we all need good health. If you want to start a business, first identify a problem worth solving.

The second cord of business; identify or create a solution to the problem. This is where things get interesting, finding a solution to the identified problem. Finding a solution to the identified problem does not require a very high IQ. In fact, having a lower IQ does not put you at a disadvantage. Average minds tend to not over-think things, which can be a good thing. Solutions need to be simple and logical. Remember the old adage; "simplicity is the hallmark of sophistication. Your customer should not require 2 years of training to use your solution. That being said; there are some solutions that require a high IQ to create.

There are inventions and technological gadgets that have such clever programming and wizardry to them that only a genius can create. What I am trying to say is that we need both high and lower IQs to create solutions to problems.

When identifying a solution there are two routes you can take;

1. **Create a unique solution.**

2. **Find an existing solution and sell that.**

Each avenue has its pros and cons. creating a unique solution may happen in a moment of inspiration which is generally followed by long hours of perspiration in development and testing, getting authorities' approval where applicable, etc.

Using an existing solution/product is comparatively easier because you skip the development phase and go straight to marketing the product. Either path is profitable and can be very rewarding when the solution does solve a problem to the satisfaction of your customer.

The third and equally important strand to the cord is; identifying a market niche that is willing to spend money to have the problem solved.

Let me tell you a story. I grew up in Africa and in the 80s and early 90s when I was still a kid, most people in our community had normal weight. As they got wealthier they began to put on more weight. Eventually, people believed that putting on weight was a sign of wealth, well-being, health, and happiness. I recall some family members striving to put on extra weight; they took vitamin supplements and extra food portions in order to add some heft. As a matter of fact, plus-size women were considered to be the most attractive. Diseases like High Blood pressure were called; "illnesses for the wealthy". If anybody tried to sell weight-loss products at that time, I don't think anybody would buy it. Simply because; even though being overweight is a problem and most of the people had that problem; our community did not consider it a problem. The mindset was all wrong; It would have been like landing in an alternate universe where things are opposite. Things changed eventually, people realized the serious repercussions of being over-weight and now more and more people are trying to stay lean.

What makes an identified problem and identified solution to make sense is a customer who is willing to pay money for the solution because they want the problem gone. If the customer doesn't think the problem is worth solving, you have no business.

Generally, a customer will buy a solution for any of the following three reasons;

1. **To save money or time.**

2. **To make money or time.**

3. **To feel good about themselves.**

When obesity was the in-thing in my country in the 80s and early 90s, selling food that induces weight gain made people feel good about themselves for some freaky reason. Thankfully now, losing weight and being healthy is valued. Worldwide, the weight-loss industry is worth billions of dollars because losing excess weight makes people look good and feel good about themselves and it saves them money on medical bills, furthermore, it gives them time by enabling them to live longer.

If the targeted market niche realizes your solution saves them money or time they will buy it. The same happens if your product or solution creates income for your customers, you have a business.

The three-strand cord of business once again;

1. **Identify a problem.**

2. **Identify/create a solution to the problem.**

3. **A market niche willing to pay for the solution to the problem.**

CHAPTER 5
Seven cycles to prosperity formula

So you've picked your investment and things are underway. If you're lucky the profits have started trickling in, if you're blessed; they are pressed down, shaken together and running over. Now how do you build an empire from your humble beginnings?

I will do my best to explain the concept behind the *"seven cycles to prosperity"*. In my opinion, it is one of the most natural ways to grow anything as I will explain later how nature uses it. The whole earth has in essence been populated using this simple formula, for most species; humans included.

I will start by telling a story I saw on television a few years ago and then proceed from there.

Once upon a time, there was a great Chinese emperor who had a son he loved very much. As years went by a time came when war broke out and the emperor sent his dear son, his great Generals and finest warriors he had off to war.

Unfortunately, the emperor's son was killed during one battle and even though they won the war the emperor was so heartbroken at the loss of his son that he was no longer the same man. His Generals and wise men tried to help him get over the grief but none succeeded.

One day, one of the wise men came to the emperor with what is today known as the game of chess and explained to the emperor that the game simulates battle situations and the idea is to strategically outwit the opponent's army.

The emperor used the same battle tactics he had used in the battle that took his son's life and for the first time found closure for his grieving heart. In gratitude the emperor offered to give the wise man whatever he would ask for; gold, silver anything he desired. The wise man declined the offer to take a reward from the grateful emperor but the king would not hear of it.

Finally, the wise man said; "alright your majesty, take the chessboard and put one grain of rice on the first square. Then put double that number on the next square, double the number of grains from the second square on the third and keep putting double the amount each square until you fill the whole chessboard".

The emperor was ecstatic, how could the wise man ask for such a small thing of him. He ordered the men from the royal granary to do as the wise man had asked. It wasn't long before they all realized what an enormous amount of rice they would have to give the wise man by the time they reached the 64th square on the board. The wise man knew the power of exponential growth.

Why did I throw in such a story; sometimes the lessons we learn from stories leave a much more lasting impression than stated facts. For example; tell a child, "don't take candy from strangers" or tell them the Hansel and Gretel story of the gingerbread house; see which one sticks.

Why is it that we have seen such a huge rise in network marketing over the past two decades? The answer is simple; the formula of exponential growth.

A network marketing company will say to its members who are in essence customers; but why be stingy with fancy titles. Call them business partners.

"If you will buy [X amount] once every month and you recruit 2 other people to buy the same [X amount] you will qualify for Y amount percentage in reward. If you help those 2 recruits each get other 2 recruits and they each buy [X amount] each month those recruits will also qualify for Y amount in reward.

One thing is emphasized; duplication. In other words; one generation of customers must produce at least double in the next generation of customers and so on and so forth… sounds familiar with the story of the wise man and the chessboard?

Now, now calm down before you go up in arms; there is nothing illegal about growing a business like that, it is simply a very clever bunch of guys employing an age-old formula for multiplicity that has always existed in nature.

Rewards from Network marketing companies may vary, the speed of multiplication may also vary but the formula stays the same. That said, my heart goes out to all those who were promised the moon but ended up shoveling dirt before finally calling it quits. But the truth of the matter is that the formula works, you just need to be on the right end of it.

Many will argue about ethics and all that, let me just say am not defending network marketing in all its forms; I am merely pointing out the driving engine at the core of its growth; exponential growth formula.

Let's turn to nature; think of bacteria. A single lonely cell will use its energy to split into 2 cells. Those 2 cells split into double that number, 4 split into 8, then 16, 32, 64 and so on. Before you know it, there is a multitude of cells. It all starts with one cell.

What does all this have to do with your financial prosperity you may ask?

Let's say you have invested $1000 in a business, you make a net profit of 100% [not something that normally happens but bear with me for the sake of the example].

You start with $1000, after trading you have $2000 [your investment principal + net profit.] You reinvest the $2000 and let's say the rabbit's foot is really working for you and somehow you manage to double your money, now you have $4000.

If you repeat the process at least 7 times it will look something like this:

$1000 - $2000 - $4000 - $8000 - $16,000 - $32,000 - $64,000 - $128,000

Think of it this way; every time you double your investment a cycle is complete. You want to do at least seven complete cycles. Don't stop at cycle number seven you can continue and make it 12 cycles of prosperity if you want; it's about the principal of methodical wealth building. In the example above, if you double it three more times your portfolio will have $1,024,000. Not bad huh?

I have been using this strategy for a while now and I've found it to be the most realistic and achievable goal not only for me but also for most people.

Growth may be fast for others, very slow for others but as long as you are able to reach the cycle goals you will make steady progress. Like they say, building wealth is not a sprint race; it's like a marathon. What I have found to be true is that money has a way of flocking to those who know how to breed it. I suppose the Holy Scripture holds true; ***"to him who has more will be given, and he shall have more abundance: but to him who does not have even the little he has will be taken away from him." Matthew 13:12.*** Why else do people say; "the rich get richer while the poor get poorer".

Let's say, your net profit margin is 10% and it will take repeating the process several times to get to double the investment, do it at your pace don't rush it. There is an old Chinese proverb; **"do not fear slow progress, only fear standing still"**.

So how does this formula work with us humans? Think of it this way. Let's say you are married, imagine drawing a family tree of your parents and ancestors up to seven generations before now. How many people will it be on both sides?

I took the liberty of drawing up a family tree diagram to illustrate:

7 Generational family tree:

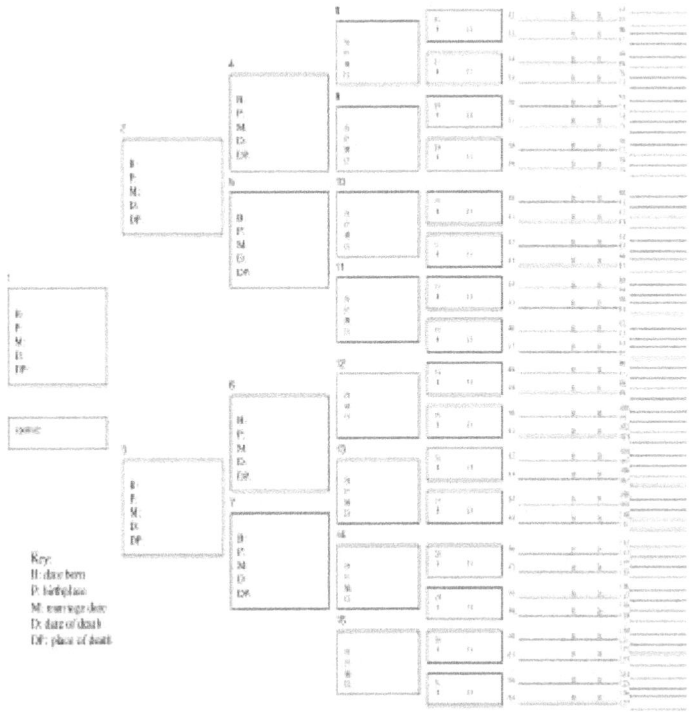

That's a lot of folks. And to think we are just counting the couples giving birth to only one child. If we added 3 children to each couple and we would not have enough paper for the tree.

I love nature's way; it's more… natural. Of course, there are other ways to multiply finances and they absolutely work. I just love the sound of the words "double your money".

Why did I pick the number seven? I remember an old trick we used to play in school; take a sheet of paper and dare each other to fold it in half more than seven times. The first fold was easy, so was the second and third. By the fifth half-folding, things were getting more difficult. Normally nobody could fold the paper in half more than seven times. Why was that? By the seventh fold you are trying to fold 256 layers of paper. Seven cycles of double multiply your initial investment two hundred and fifty-six times.

Getting your business to be a profitable venture is a whole new subject, however. It will require skill, energy, a lot more learning and hard work. It may take some adjusting to your environment and a host of other important things that are needed to make a business work. The bottom line; do what needs to be done to make an investment work. Set up proper systems, market the product, and be in touch with your customers because great businesses survive on repeat businesses.

Read some books on starting a business; get a mentor to make sure there is money flowing into the business then use the 7 cycles to Prosperity formula to build your wealth. I am convinced that any profitable business venture can create wealth.

Please also keep in mind the old wise saying; "Don't keep all your eggs in one basket" or as the Holy Bible so aptly put it; ***"Give a portion to seven, and also to eight; for thou knowest not what evil shall be upon the earth."*** ***Ecclesiastes 11:2.***

While there is power in focus, sometimes it pays to invest in others just in case some unforeseen calamity shows its ugly head. What I've personally always done is to first establish an income source/business, consolidate it; making it self-sustaining. Once it has enough momentum to keep going I put my profits into another opportunity that looks profitable.

Usually, at this point the temptation is to roll the dice and see how things pan out; but it's important to do proper research. I make sure I understand the investment opportunity. If it takes some complex formula to prove profitability, it may not be what it seems to be. Simple is best. Repeat after me; "simplicity is the hallmark of sophistication".

If there are too many variables that are out of your control a dream investment can quickly turn into a nightmare. I don't know of many success stories that came at the roll of the dice with the exception of winning the lottery of course. But then many Lottery winners end up right where they started… broke. If you've ever heard a lottery winner who has doubled their money after winning please share his contacts; not only is he the luckiest man alive… he's a lucky charm. I wouldn't mind some of that luck rubbing off on me.

My import is that; success comes from deliberate choice and hard work. There may be a moment of inspiration but it's the long hours of perspiration that make a dream come true.

CHAPTER 6
Digging trenches: make others' success your own

In this chapter we're going to deal with entrepreneur mentality. Now the title may suggest that I am well versed in warfare but to speak the truth I have never been in any war not to say the least any of the two world wars so I cannot base this chapter on any war of the past century. I am however going to narrate an ancient war story from the Holy Bible. You may notice that I have used the good book quite often in the chapters of this book. Well, let's just say I am a big fan of buying wisdom wholesale. Why read a few excerpts when I can help myself with a whole buffet of ancient wisdom.

The scene is set in ancient Palestine long after the time of King David. The whole kingdom of Israel had long passed from the hands of David's descendants. Only Judah was left to the house of David, the other 10 tribes had formed a nation called "Israel" with Samaria as their capital city.

King Jehoshaphat was on the throne of Judah, with the King's city – Jerusalem as his capital.

The son of the deceased wicked King Ahab, King Jehoram invited king Jehoshaphat and the king of Edom to join him wage war against the king of Moab. They start off on this massive military campaign and I guess due to poor planning, they ran out of water seven days into the journey.

Not a single drop of water for the men or the large herd of cattle that followed them; too bad corn beef hadn't been invented yet. After some back and forth King Jehoshaphat suggested they call upon the Prophet Elisha for a consultation.

This was his advice; "2Kings 3:16 And he said, Thus saith the LORD, Make this valley full of ditches. 17 For thus saith the LORD, Ye shall not see wind, neither shall ye see rain; yet that valley shall be filled with water, that ye may drink, both ye, and your cattle, and your beasts. 18 And this is but a light thing in the sight of the LORD: he will deliver the Moabites also into your hand."

Back in Malawi, we have an old saying which goes; **"water never forgets its path"**. The man Elisha understood that the army was in a valley and they needed water. They had some options before them; wait for rain or dig wells. There was however a third option prepare for rain that will fall somewhere else.

By digging trenches in the valley; all the rain that would fall on any of the mountains and highlands would find its way to their doorstep… well trenches. They anticipated abundance outside of their circumstance and sure as an egg, the next morning there was more water than they needed. That is the power of foresight, mentorship, hope, and preparation.

It's important to choose your mentors wisely. There are people who have the ability to see things before they happen. You need such people as advisors. You will need to do the digging of course; dig as deep as you need to. Good advice calls for quick and decisive action. What good is great advice if nothing is done about it?

So many people hear of opportunities but procrastinate to do the necessary work or to make the investment. They wake up one morning, to find a deluge of water running past their front door into the neighbor's trench. Hasty digging ensues but alas! Muddy puddles lay all over the place. Most if not all opportunities are best-taken advantage of before everyone knows about it. By the time you see the bandwagon, it's already too late. Opportunity indeed has a big backside; that's why it looks bigger going than when coming.

Many people expect that their advancement will only happen if their circumstance changes. Many times someone else's good fortune causes your prosperity. Think of the gold rush in the old days. Folk rushed to claim their portion of the gold yielding territory but gold was not the only fortune to be made. Tradesmen made a fortune quicker than some of those miners. With the miners busy in the mines, farmers had people to sell food to. Learn to see patterns in other people's progress and lifestyle advancements; make a way to supply what they need and you will have yourself a business.

If we think like that, it will eliminate all thoughts of jealousy and envy. Someone else's blessing and prosperity is your potential income if you can position yourself well, dig your trenches and dig them deeply indeed.

What if you are an employee and have no business acumen whatsoever?

The underlying principle of business is basically solving someone else's problem. How much you get paid depends on what problem you solve. That said, we have a lot of people who seem to underestimate the power of an employee. Think about it; the employee sector is the one sector which upholds all the other sectors; small to large scale businesses depend on the employee sector to make their fortune. Governments depend on the employment sector simply because employees are the ones who earn consistently. Earnings may be smaller but consistent and consistency is the cornerstone to prosperity. In my opinion and experience; an employee who has the habit of saving at least 10% of their income can actually get wealthy at a considerable pace simply by becoming a problem solver for those who are committed to problem-solving; Invest in entrepreneurs' businesses. I am not talking about just blindly throwing money into the stock market or bankrolling your nephews magic rocks business. If as an employee, you actively look for business ideas with great potential and you do your homework to make sure your interests and investment are secure. You can make a fortune and the beauty of it is that you already have an existing source of income so you can focus on doubling your investment at least seven times and you are wealthy. The main challenge is to make sure your thirst doesn't get bigger than your quest. Once the profits start rolling in, you will feel like buying that nice car or house but instead of rewarding yourself right away, delay the gratification until you have finished the seven cycles. When you get to the end you will not only have abundance but you will have respect for yourself and you will have mastered money and your own emotions. There will be pressure from within and from those around you, that is for sure; the presence of money has a way of attracting such.

CHAPTER 7
Get in the flow

Having talked about the need for strategic positioning and anticipating opportunities, I think it is only fitting that I add this small chapter about financial flow.

If there is a problem that can cripple or even kill a business it is lack of cash flow. By that I mean; money should come in and out of the business. Of course, to be successful more money should come in than money going out. Now how do you get to a place where you have a lot of financial traffic?

I said earlier that; it is better when things naturally flow. I once heard life coach and motivational speaker Roger Hamilton speaking on getting in the flow of nature. Imagine you want to have wild animals at your business place. Being in Africa it's easier to imagine because we have more tree jungles than concrete jungle here.

There are a couple of ways to go about it.

1. You can build a resort and build a zoo on your premises. You will need to file a mountain of paper work with the government, take on the responsibility of feeding all the animals which have different diets mind you. After a substantial investment you will have your wildlife resort. Guests will come and well you have yourself a nice spot. Expensive to build and even more expensive to run but a nice place none the less.

2. The second option would be to build your resort at any location of your choice and as part of your service, have tours by vehicle. Your only investment is not as much as in the first scenario but you will need to have vehicles to transport your guests into the wild for them to see some animals. Sure it will require hiring expert animal trackers and studying animal habits to perfectly time when and where to find which animals but at least you don't have to worry about feeding the animals.

3. Or you could take the third option; find a watering hole where the animals go to drink and build a resort nearby. Once your resort opens, you never have to search for wild animals or transport your guests anywhere. Nor do you need to feed the animals. Instead of going to the wild animals, they come to you. Well, they come to the watering hole where you are. Of course you may need to be careful not to feed your guests to some

carnivorous beasts but you are otherwise fine. You have entered the flow of nature.

There are many times when people start a business and try to take people out of their natural flow in order to support the business. Many times it doesn't work out so well or it works at huge expense because there is no flow. The whole point of business is to serve your customers; making their life easier. Life is in essence a flow. Just think about it, the blood in our bodies keep us alive by flowing. Air flows in and out of our bodies, the same with water. The day you need an external element to keep the flow in your body going [dialysis for example] you know that something is wrong. Life is a flow, money is a flow. The easiest and most natural way to do business is to get yourself in the path of money and you will never have to chase and track it down. Take a look at almost all successful businesses in the world; they positioned themselves next to the watering hole. Whether it's online shopping, transportation, food processing, communication, restaurants, hotels, schools; they all found a place in the flow of man's natural environment. There are times when a good business idea needs a little tweaking to make it work. Have you ever heard the business mantra; "location, location, location". I guess they meant; "find the flow, find the flow, find the flow".

CHAPTER 8
Bouncing back from failure

Let's say for some reason things went sideways and you find yourself flat on your face; your investment has failed. If it's painful, you are in the right frame of mind don't give up hope. To build finances you need a level of mental fortitude that can carry you through such times. Sure it stings like salt on a fresh wound; you may not feel like getting out of bed the next day but it's all part of the journey; don't lose hope.

Depending on one's personality; reactions may vary. Others internalize which is not the best solution by the way while others externalize; a healthier alternative if you do it in a healthy way.

I have personally never lost a huge amount of money but I have been flat broke before so I have been there and back again in a manner of speaking. What I'd recommend is to accept that the money is gone; mistakes were made, learn the lessons that need learning from the experience and move on.

First thing to do is to plant another seed as soon as possible. What do I mean by this; continue the practice of saving at least 10% of your income. The moment you have your first 10% in your savings you are no longer flat broke and that is a good place to stand. Here is the beauty of cycles; they come around. There is a good side to "what goes around comes around" after all.

Once you've built up enough savings repeat the seven cycle process [minus the mistakes from the previous investment of course]. Some mistakes and attitudes are like clockwork; they always bring out the same results time after time. At least you experienced it firsthand.

Don't get me wrong, there are other circumstances where bad things happen to good business people. Political changes, war, divorce, crime the list is endless. Those are things that are not the fault of the business owner, still plant another seed.

Think of it as a new beginning on steroids. You are not starting from scratch. You have contacts from your previous endeavor; you now know what you did not know the first time around. This time around, it may take less time to gain progress than the previous time because you have experience on your side.

Here is one of my favorite scriptures on the subject;

Job 14:7 KJV: "For there is hope for a tree, if it be cut down, that it will sprout again, and that the tender branch thereof will not cease. 8 Though the root thereof wax old in the earth, and the stock thereof die in the ground; 9 Yet through the scent of water it will bud, and bring forth boughs like a plant.

If your tree has been cut down, don't burn the stump; look for water or at least wait for rain season… there is still hope.

CHAPTER 9
The power of resolution

There is very little that can be achieved without strong resolve in this world. We all must individually come to the quality decision to take financial success; to make it happen. I think the saddest sight I have ever seen is that of people waiting for success. There are people who spend their lives waiting in line for their turn at the good life; I blame it on society's inculcation on fairness. We give each other turns to play with the single toy on the playground; it's the polite thing to do.

The day I realized that they are not handing out success is the day I stepped away from the queue. If success was being handed out, older people would be more successful because they would be at the front of the line, plus they have seniority. Success is taken not given out. If you haven't succeeded yet, it's not because your turn hasn't come yet; it's because you haven't taken it yet. It doesn't just happen; you make it happen.

It all starts with making a resolution to succeed. I know we are all used to making New Year resolutions and we all know how many of those are kept and seen through to fruition. Look no further than the gym bag that's been sitting next to the door for the last six months. It is strange to note that in the jubilant mood of New Year's Eve resolutions are made to do certain things but we don't follow through on most of them.

On the other end of the scale, in our everyday, routine mundane lives we encounter all sorts of emotions and there are moments when we decide to do or no longer do certain things and years later we are resolute in our commitment.

For example; someone breaks your heart and you resolve to never interact with them and years later you haven't said a word to that loved one. Though it may have come out of a bad experience, it gives me hope to know that each and every one of us has the ability to make and keep a resolution. I recon under the right mental condition we can be decisive and resolute. Perhaps the trick is in picking moments for making resolutions. Personally I don't believe there is a particular season for great decision and resolution making but I know this for a fact; you don't need to be excited or in a good mood to make a great resolution.

At the age of 37, I found myself unemployed, without any money except for the $100 from my 10% savings. We could no longer afford to pay rent so we ended up with my wife's parents for the second time. The date was November 7th 2016. On that day in the midst of the dark and gloom, I decided that I will be a millionaire by the age of 40. It was a simple resolution which consisted of six steps.

1. Get a job.

2. Save at least 10% of my income.

3. Use my other talents to create income.

4. Minimize expenses.

5. Invest in safe and profitable business ventures.

6. Repeat steps 2 to 5.

I did not find a full time job unfortunately, but when life throws lemon at you, grab the salt because tequila shots are on the way. Don't just think "lemonade", life deserves something better to make a toast with.

I looked for a potential business and started investing my savings in safe and profitable business ventures. Now don't get me wrong; when I say "safe" investments I do not mean low interest stocks and bonds. Safe means, I took the time to research the market, I saw a customer base for the product and I invested in items with redeemable value such that if things don't go as planned. I could sell the items at cost and get my principle back.

It has been a practice of mine to do that since the demise of my first business venture. Let me put it this way' it's great to advertise and all but if the advertising budget is more than the actual value of your sellable stock, you may be in for a rough ride if the advertising campaign doesn't roll out as planned.

Now, how do you make strong enough resolutions? In my case it was simply being frustrated by my current lot in life that drove me to decide that I want to get out of it. Most of the best resolutions I have ever made came at what I call crossroad moments. Such moments have usually not been happy excited times, nor were they moments of depression. It seems extremes on the emotion scale produce resolutions which are clouded by either joy or sadness. There is need to be able to get to that mid point where thoughts are clear, emotions have settled down and you see things as they are not as you wish them to be during excitement or as how fear exaggerates them in moments of sadness and depression.

Am not sure what to call that place exactly, but when you get there; you know it. Here is a hint; it doesn't happen at parties.

CHAPTER 10
THE LEARNING CURVE

One of the most frustrating things in life is to succeed and then find yourself stuck at one level. It's not that you are failing but you feel you are not succeeding either. Call it stagnation, hitting the glass ceiling, stuck in a rutt; it has such an effect on the human brain that often we seek answers from our past experiences and victories but for some reason, none of those answers fit. It's almost how it felt to be a growing kid when one day, you put on your favorite pair of shoes and for some reason, they just won't fit. There is only one reason for this; we all outgrow our current level at some point.

On my journey, I have had to come to terms and made peace with the fact that what got me here will not take me through the next level of where I am going.

It can be a scary thought because no matter how courageous and adventurous you can be when starting something new; the time will come when the current new thing or level will be your old level. Guess what, to move to the next new thing, level or season as it were; your current knowledge, experience, and awareness cannot take you there.

Think of it like this; a fertilized chicken egg will grow a chick inside its shell. There are enough sustenance and protection for the growing chick throughout the development phase. As this phase gets closer and closer to its end, the chick gets bigger and the eggshell no longer has enough space for the little bird inside.

When D-day comes either the eggshell gets cracked to release the little chick to its next season or the eggshell remains intact aborting the very life it has so caringly nurtured from the beginning. (not the greatest of examples but you get the point). Many times people hit a ceiling after a period of great success and suddenly it feels like nothing works anymore. Why is that? Generally, it's because one phase has come to an end and another phase is meant to start. Your inner self knows it, that's why you feel like a fish out of water.

As we grow, it's almost like our minds have boundaries. I like to think of it as a glass dome. The mind sets achievable boundaries but lets you see beyond its current boundaries as far as you choose to see. When you get to the edge of the dome, the only way to get to what you can see it by breaking the current dome. This means you learn new skills, move to a higher level of awareness and change your way of operating.

Let's say for example you run a business selling products and you are personally involved in selling. Because you are very passionate about what you do, you are not only the business owner but also the top salesperson of your company.

As a result of your hard work and dedication, your business is making hundreds of thousands of Rands. However, you feel it is time for the business to hit millions in revenue. At this point you have a choice to make; will you travel more, work longer hours than you already do, weekends and why not, sacrifice some family time. Or will you dedicate more of your time mentoring the other salespeople in your business and headhunting good salespeople?

The two choices require two totally different mindsets, actions, and attitudes. One reinforces the shell while the other breaks the mould. There is an old saying; "if you want to go fast go alone, if you want to go far take company". Ironically sometimes to go far you must first go fast, and then pick up company along the way.

The trick is recognizing when it's time to go fast and when it's time to slow down enough to pick up company. Please take note that I say slow down not come to a dead stop. Things that are in a state of inertia always tend to want to stay in that state, the idea is to keep moving.

When it comes to making more money, there may be times when we hit a wall (it happens to the best of us). Maybe to get through it you may need to move around to other businesses and enterprises; whatever you need to do. At the end of the day such times are moments that force our mind to grow. The expansion is actually a breaking down of one mindset to enter a new with its new parameters, strategies and required skill sets.I played video games back in the day and I remember well how as you advanced to higher game levels, it got harder, villains were more resilient and you had to learn new patterns of play to counter enemy attacks but in the end; we adapted and we finished game level after game level.

Remember the old Microsoft saying about the Squid and the Dinosaur; the one evolved the other went extinct.

CHAPTER 11
100+ LESSONS OF A LIFETIME

I thought I should end with some of the lessons that I have learnt in the past 39 years; hopefully, you will find a nugget or two to help you along the way. They are laid out in no particular order of importance but each has helped me in my endeavors. Some of the lessons I learnt from bad experiences are usually the case but other lessons I was smart enough to learn without feeling the sting of negative Consequences.

1 Don't get greedy.

2 Be wary of those that renegotiate after shaking on it; the new terms seldom come from a sincere place.

3 Do the math; if it doesn't add up on paper, it most likely won't work out in real life.

4 Pay attention to the numbers.

5 If you're an artist; be a great artist but do not neglect to learn the art of money… it's what brought you into the industry.

6 Be hopeful.

7 Love those who love you back.

8 Never abandon those who love you for those you like.

9 Momentum is easy to kill but hard to resuscitate.

10 Take care of your body, mind, soul, and spirit; you only have one of each.

11 If you must choose between health and wealth, choose health; there is always another way to get wealth, the same cannot be said about health.

12 Money is important.

13 Love and appreciate family and loved ones, they are the most likely to stick with you when the world turns its back on you.

14 Anything can happen.

15 Important things may not be fun to do, but you will have fun when you've done them.

16 You are the prophet of your own life.

17 Time and opportunity come to all men, including you.

18 See a doctor and keep your dentist's appointment.

19 You can get rich.

20 Poverty is a choice.

21. Never insult a business partner or colleague by sending them on a fool's errand. If you value their time, they will value yours.

22. Choose a mentor carefully.

23. Mentor someone else.

24. Make sure you always invest in things with redeemable value.

25. If you failed once don't lose heart, keep going.

26. Do not read financial books only but history, poetry, and fiction. The flame of passion is fed by words.

27. Laugh.

28. Smile.

29. Cry when sad but don't cry forever.

30. Accept that some people will like you and others will not like you.

31. Regret is the greatest thief of time.

32. Acquire some general knowledge and current news. It helps you stay relevant, makes for good conversation and it helps you understand standup comedy (if that sort of stuff is important to you).

33. Dance.

34. Have a favorite song, even if you only know the tune; it will lift your spirits.

35. You should love investing more than you love a job; investment is a faithful servant that will pay you and your children's children for generations to come. A job is a fickle mistress which will pay only you, that too conditionally for a few years.

36. Protect your investment.

37. Seek to always increase your earning power; it's the only cure to small living.

38. Winning: you can win by winning and you can lose by losing. It's also possible to lose by winning just as much as it is possible to win by losing. The point is to always find a way to win.

39. There are more ways to get paid than just cash; master trading.

40. If someone owes you money and can't pay you; find a way to get paid that doesn't involve cash. You will get value and you will keep a friend; that's a win-win.

41. Taking offense closes you off to divine possibilities; keep a pure heart.

42. Respect your elders. You may have more money than them but you do not have their years, experience and wisdom.

43. Think, think again…keep thinking.

44. All great ideas evolve; embrace the evolution.

45. Embrace change like a dear friend.

46. "Meet with triumph and disaster and treat those two impostors just the

same" Rudyard Kipling

47. What is spoken cannot be unspoken.

48. Don't just speak; say something.

49. We all basically have the same building blocks; time, thoughts and words. Choose your thoughts and words carefully; time is limited.

50. Courage can be borrowed.

51. Play with your children and they will pray with you.

52. Watching television is basically watching someone else busy at their job.

53. If the mind is strong, nurture it and for goodness sake build the body to house it well.

54. Almost anything can be learnt.

55. If you can't do it slowly, you will not do it fast. *Chinese proverb*

56. The world is getting smaller; don't neglect going across the street to greet an old friend.

57. There is room for one more book; fancy writing it?

58. Saving money is the starting point; investment is what makes you wealthy.

59. Take responsibility for your life; failure and success depend on your actions or lack thereof.

60. Never procrastinate.

61. Empathize with other people's problems; your next big business may come from solving one of them.

62. Things are not always what they seem to be.

63. There is no self-made man; we are all products of someone else's efforts to pass on values. Don't be too stingy to share the lessons.

64. It's amazing how much good you do to yourself when you help someone else succeed.

65. Lift up other people and you will stand taller, push down others and you stand shorter… and they will take you down with them.

66. Ask good questions, they determine the answers you get.

67. Contrary to popular belief, nature has abundance.

68. We all see the future; we hold it in our arms every day – our children.

69. Consequences come by default.

70. Learn a lesson and move on to the next lesson.

71. We all have to start over sometimes.

72. Start somewhere, end somewhere else.

73. You may start from the bottom but get out of the basement as soon as possible.

74. Delayed gratification shows mastery over self.

75. There is always somebody better than you at something; the trick is to learn to live confidently with your "self".

76. Television is more captivating than radio but the pictures are better on radio and I dare say the pictures are even much better in picture-less books.

77. Never put the cart before the ox. The ox is good at pulling but not so great at pushing – let your investments create your lifestyle, not the other way around.

78. First cultivate your field, and then build your own house.

79. Take lots of pictures now even when you don't feel fabulous; that opinion of your "self-image" will change in a couple of years.

80. Freedom is priceless.

81. Follow peace.

82. If something drains you of energy, let it go.

83. Pray even if you never learnt how to; it's an act of faith not an art to flaunt.

84. Working hard brings lots of good luck; laziness brings a tone of misfortune.

85. Losing is not for losers though they do it more often than most; we all face defeat occasionally.

86. Losers make less or no mistakes compared to winners.

87. If you find yourself stuck, step back; listen to a mentor or read a book. The situation may not change but you will change; your consciousness will increase. Increased consciousness is the birthplace of great breakthrough.

88. Learn to whistle; even with no natural musical talent, you will never suck at any song.

89. Pick your battles.

90. To get out of debt; first focus on increasing your income, then take control of your expenditure.

91. When you get wealth; upgrade your house, clothes, cars, and lifestyle… But keep your loved ones.

92. In life there will be people who will love you for no reason just as there will be people who will hate you for no reason: choose which group you want on your side.

93. Fame and fortune: Fame may make you wealthy if you can use it wisely. Wealth on the other hand will easily make you famous and you won't care much about fame.

94. If you got rich from fame the temptation is to compromise to please the fans: Own the fame, don't let fame owns you.

95. A big payday is great but it is regular customers that will make you rich and will keep you rich.

96. In business, focus on what is working and keep working it.

97. First feed the hunting dog then you will have a feast for your cute house pets.

98. Never lose yourself. Some things and other people can be replaced but who you are is irreplaceable.

99. Time is more valuable than money… it's priceless.

100. Taking risks is good, risky living is a bad idea.

101. Have a good pair of shoes; your feet and knees will carry you for life, they deserve to be treated kindly.

102 Learn business principles, and then learn to trust your instincts. There are plenty of things books cannot teach you.

103. Give heed to re-occurring dreams; there is no truer mirror for your spirit, soul, and body.

104. Dream big then get up and build them.

105. Build big in small manageable portions.

106. Humility is being proud of who you are without feeling the need to bring somebody else down, just so that you can look bigger.

107. Pain and suffering are part of life BUT avoid and end unnecessary pain and suffering.

108. If you provide what people need you will prosper anywhere.

109. If your children have to start where you started (struggling financially) you haven't done your family much good.

110. Be a gathering giver or giving gatherer.

111. Never become a victim of your own success.

112. Inexperience breeds cruelty.

113. No matter how colorful you are as a caterpillar you will be more beautiful as a butterfly; embrace the metamorphosis.

114. After learning all financial principles and practicing them; understand that there is only one reason you will get wealthy; catching your big break!

115. Don't let money stop you from getting wealth.

116. Selling on credit can potentially ruin a business.

117. Being cautious with money does not show a lack of faith, rather it is a display of maturity and sense of responsibility.

118. Cheap wine is some rather expensive vinegar.

119. When doing something impossible, first I ask; WHAT?

Then I ask WHY? WHEN? Followed by WHO? Finally, I ask; HOW?

120. When life throws you lemons, either fish is on the menu or Tequila shots are on the way… perspective is everything.

121. When life throws you lemons, make grape juice. (You always have a choice). No need to recycle the crap life throws at you; live from your creativity.

122. Stand alone if you must.

123. In school I learnt how to count, and then I had to learn to make my life count.

124. You will not have the time to… if you do not take the time to…

125. Every leader's worst nightmare: followers that refuse to take directions and followers who will only comply as long as the follow from in front.

126.Sometimes there is a reason why there is no shortcut.

127.Pay your dues.

128.I am not a winner because you failed, am a winner because WE are succeeding.

129.Do your most important work when you are most fresh, then attend to other things and other people.

130.Never set low goals; it usually takes the same amount of faith and time to achieve both low and high goals.

131.Appreciate your parents, love and honour your spouse, cherish your children and keep a good friend.

132.Travel; see new places and embrace new ideas.

133.There is only one problem with a self-centered life… you are lonely no matter how many people surround you.

134.A song can help you declare with conviction things you wouldn't otherwise have the confidence to say.

135.Family is important.

136.When it comes to life, don't beat about the bush; the timeline is straight.

137.In the business arena, time and again you will get a bloody nose. Wipe off the blood BUT do not medicate the pain, do not sedate yourself and do not band aid; you need the pain on the rebound. It reminds you that you're still here.

138.Match your effort with your desire.

139.Hate evil with the same fervency you love righteousness.

140.We all need other people.

141.Freedom of the seas is enslavement to the map and compass.

142.Always have something to sell.

143 Life owes you neither a livelihood nor happiness; you owe it to yourself to make the most of the time you have been given.

PROLOQUE

This book is dedicated to every employee who has ever worked long and hard in the hope of securing a bright future for their family. So many times we hear people bad mouth the employment sector and look down upon ordinary hard working people but if you come to think of it; the masses in the employment sector literary lifts the commercial sector on its shoulders.

I have come to believe that an individual with a job has the raw material and the power to do anything. You may be working for someone else at the moment but every month a deposit of seed comes into your hands. With this seed, you can grow a rain forest that will end the drought of poverty that is threatening to plague your family for generations to come.

Money is a form of power, with a little you can do very little with a lot you can have a great impact. Cumulatively over a lifetime of employment, an individual will have received hundreds of thousands or millions of dollars in monthly income. The only problem is that the income does not come as a lump sum; time stretches it out, scattering or spreading it out over years of labor.

What if you can learn to slow down time enough to crystallize deposits of wealth? I am talking about deliberately and purposefully building financial strength regardless of your current circumstances. It all starts with desire and a choice to do it.

Imagine being able to build using only two steps. What if I told you that these two simple steps can help you build the financial muscle you desire? I say "simple" not easy. The steps are simple because they are not complicated. Not easy because it will require some hard work. The words "easy" and "money" should not be in the same sentence as far as I know.

I sincerely hope that this book will illuminate your path, inspire your soul to awaken, stir you up to arise and build and show you that you have an open invitation to the feast of wealth that you have up to this point only watched with longing eyes and cracked lips as others partook of its bounty. There is more than enough to go around.

The end